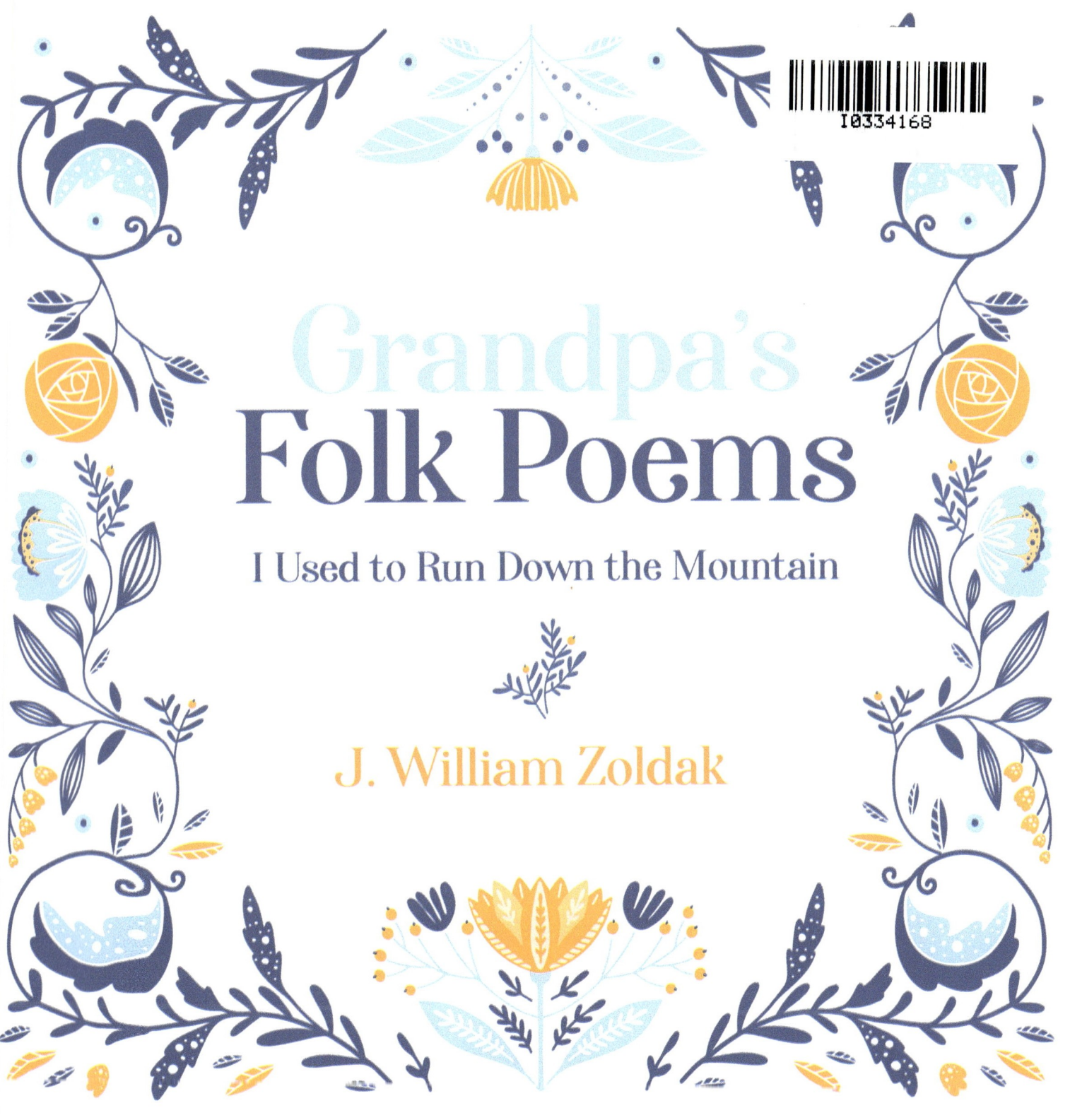

Grandpa's Folk Poems

I Used to Run Down the Mountain

J. William Zoldak

ALSO BY J. WILLIAM ZOLDAK

Grandpa's Christmas Tree Story
Grandpa's Deer Story
Grandpa's Memories of Main STreet
Grandpa's Day at the Circus
Grandpa's Bumble Bee Story

Grandpa's Folk Poems
I Used to Run Down the Mountain

Hardcover ISBN: 978-1-0881-1476-6
Paperback ISBN: 978-1-0881-1492-6

©2023 J. William Zoldak

ALL RIGHTS RESERVED.

No part of this publication may be translated, reproduced or transmitted in any form without prior permission in writing from the publisher.

Photo Credits: All photos property of the author with the addition of the following:
The Master Hunter ©Pixabay, The Winds on Secore's Hill ©Pixabay
Fireflies ©Pixabay, The Old Swimming Hole ©Bob McCue
The Cherry Thieves ©Misti Hobbs, Lulabelle ©Misti Hobbs
The Little Yellow Church in the Grove ©Emma Meade
A Place Called Childhood ©Pixabay, This Old Barn ©Hope Coons
The Ghost Herd ©Misti Hobbs
Folk art illustrations ©Dariia Baranova

Published by Stonehedges
OXFORD, MASSACHUSETTS

STONEHEDGES

Dear Grandchildren,

During my younger years, I spent many wonderful hours, usually early in the morning with a cup of coffee in my hand, thinking up rhyming poems. Often they were written on a scrap of paper or on the back of an envelope. These thoughts were more often than not incomplete. When it was time for me to begin my day I would slip them into one of my favorite poetry books for safe keeping. As time went on I would complete some of the poems in a more permanent form and put them in a notebook. The incomplete thoughts were either left in the poetry book or thrown in the top drawer of my dresser. I couldn't type so they were all hand written. One day a dear friend volunteered to take them and type them for me. Because in those days, there were no copying machines I only had one copy. Then in 1991 when copying machines, were available, my daughter made a few copies bound with ribbons and gave them to me as a Christmas present. Shortly thereafter I stopped writing. I'm not sure why.

After about a 20-year lapse I started writing again. At first I wondered if I could still do it, but after a while I found that I could. Some of the poems in this book are old ones that I updated, some are new ones that I created recently and some are poems that I finished from bits that I found in my old poetry books or my dresser drawer. Since my experiences are from a different era, the poems tend to reflect those times. I hope you enjoy them.

With love,
Grandpa

Grandpa's Folk Poems

I Used to Run Down the Mountain
Old Tools
Gentle Breezes
Mountain Laurel
The Master Hunter
The Old Farm Spring
The Smell of Fresh Cut Hay
Boys and Brooks
Spring Flowers
Shadows on the Garden Wall
The Old Stonewall
The Winds on Secore's Hill
Fireflies
The Old Swimming Hole
The Cherry Thieves
Lulabelle
Death of a Great Poet
Can I Go Out Fishing in Heaven?
Stray Cat
The Little Yellow Church in the Grove
Twilight on the Hudson
A Place Called Childhood
This Old Barn
The Ghost Herd
The Temple Green

I Used to Run Down the Mountain

I used to run down the mountain
Lickety-split past rock and tree.
I used to run down the mountain
So fast that I could barely see.
There were those that said I shouldn't
Be running so out of control.
I worried not for a moment;
My legs were strong, my body whole.

I used to walk down the mountain,
Following tiny paths, not straight.
I used to walk down the mountain,
At a respectable walking gait.
As I journeyed through moss and fern,
I heard all the birds sweetly sing.
It seemed that around every turn
Something lovely the path would bring.

I used to drive down the mountain
Following the old winding way.
I used to drive down the mountain,
But on the narrow road I'd stay.
I could hear the wind in the leaves
And smell scents I remember well.
I enjoyed all that nature weaves
Up and down the forest dell.

But if for one moment in time
I could choose from the former three,
I would run down the mountain
Lickety-split past rock and tree.

Old Tools On The Wall

The tools on the old barn wall
Remind us of yesteryear.
If they could talk, they'd recall
Stories we might like to hear.

The bucksaw with all its charm,
Hanging there so old and gray,
Cut firewood for the farm,
Warming family night and day.

The block and tackle up there,
With its fine ropes strong and stout,
Helped to clear the fields so fair,
Pulling all the tree stumps out.

The pitchfork used in its day,
Feeding cattle in the shed,
Helped scatter both grass and hay,
Until everyone was fed.

The Ice tongs there on the wall,
Reminds us of cooling ways,
When the ice man made his call,
Before refrigeration days.

A two man saw hangs there too,
Used to cut the big trees down
Making hardwood logs to hew,
For a cabin strong and sound.

On the wall the oxen yoke,
Worn by those beasts of burden,
Eased life for farming folk
While in their fields up turfin'.

The old scythe secure and safe
Upon the wall way up high,
A memory of mower's grace
Upon using this old scythe.

The big hay rake hanging there
May have been used long ago.
In its day it did its share
After the field had a mow.

These old tools upon the wall
May have passed beyond their prime,
But some of us may recall
Their grandeur within this rhyme.

Gentle Breezes

I love the gentle breezes
That blow – the clouds away.
I love the gentle breezes
That bring a sunny day.

I can take the thunder boomers
And nights of pelting rain
As long as cloudless mornings
Follow the storms as they wane.

I love the way the Fall leaves tumble,
Floating toward the ground,
Caught by gentle breezes
And moving without a sound.

I even like the ice and snow
When days are short and cold
As long as there are gentle breezes
To make the air brisk and bold.

The harshness of life's dark side
Can toss me to and fro
As long as gentle breezes
Within my heart doth flow.

I love the gentle breezes
That blow the clouds away.
I love the gentle breezes
That bring a sunny day.

Mountain Laurel

Numerous blossoms, pinkish white,
Deep, green heavy leaves, shining bright,
Beautifying from dawn til night,
Sweeping up the mountainside.

Sheltering deer and smaller game,
Twisting, snarling all but tame,
Always lovely just the same
Sweeping down the other side.

Covering rock and barren ground,
Holding humus and soil down,
Sending cheerfulness all around.
Scattering grace far and wide.

The Master Hunter

Old Bill Secore was a hunter,
The best there was around.
When Bill's feet touched the forest floor,
All the animals hit the ground.

The deer fled for cover.
The squirrels ran from tree to tree.
The rabbits went down under.
He even scared the bumble bee.

They never knew which way he'd turn
Or what he had in mind that day.
They only knew that he was comin',
And where they were, they couldn't stay.

There came a mass evacuation.
No sound was heard. Not a peep.
Those that had no place to hide
Penetrated the forest deep.

Now this may sound rather strange
For so many to be afraid of one,
Especially when you consider
That old Bill didn't own a gun.

His mastery of the art of hunting
Was advanced beyond belief.
He would never ever hurt his prey
For that would cause them grief.

His methods were shrewd and cunnin,
Not conventional at all.
For a while they'd escape his hand,
But eventually they all would fall.

He'd just try to catch them
And then he'd let them go,
But oh, how clever he was
With rod, rope, bough, and bow.

When the hunt was over
And victory was at his door,
He'd stand within the forest glade
And let out a joyous roar.

Then they knew the hunt was over
And they could relax once more
At least until the next time
His feet touched the forest floor.

The Old Farm Spring

Way out behind the red cow barn,
There was an old cold-water spring.
If that spring were to spin a yarn,
Oh, such tales to life it would bring.

Through the stones just above the ground,
Water from an old pipe would flow
Making a quiet, splashing sound
As it struck the puddle below.

On the shelf within the stone wall
Just above the old iron pipe,
A coconut shell there for all
Used to sip this liquid delight.

Grass mowers from out in the field
Would find rest there from their labors;
Drinking of what the spring would yield
While conversing with the neighbors.

Hired hands would often look in
On this spring they cherished so much
As they gathered the hay crop in
Using a rake, pitch fork and such.

Children roaming through from afar
Would always stop by for a taste,
Giving their young taste buds a jar,
Then moving along in great haste.

Way down at the base of the wall,
Water collected in a pond
Providing refreshment for all
The creatures both near and beyond.

After dark, the doe and the fawn,
Feeding in the meadow nearby,
Would venture over before dawn
To sample this water supply.

The farm animals drank there too,
The cattle, the sheep, and the goats
Refreshing their bodies anew
And soothing their over-parched throats.

A stranger moseying on through
Seeing an odd pipe in the wall
Might not take the time to review
Such an awesome vision he saw.

If he were to stay and reflect
Upon the wonder before him,
Then he would probably select
To come to the spring more often.

Yes, the old spring at the stone wall
Flourished on day in and day out
And for those of us who recall,
It will stay well with us, no doubt.

The Smell of Fresh Cut Hay

I love the smell of sunshine
As it dries up all the rain.
I love the smell of Lilacs,
As I wander down the lane.

But of all the smells of Spring
The one that I love the best
Is the smell of fresh cut hay,
Just after it's laid to rest.

Sometimes I come across it
While walking a rural road
To find a short time later
A meadow that's just been mowed.

And when this happens to me,
I stop there and sit awhile
As my mind meanders back
To perhaps, a country mile.

To the days when I was young
Working in the fields of hay,
Mowing, raking, and baling,
Soaking in the scent of day.

Though you may feel different
About smells you cherish much,
Until you're smelled fresh cut hay
With heaven you're out of touch.

Boys and Brooks

Brooks run shallow – brooks run deep.
Boyhood memories are bound to keep.

There stands a boy upon the shore
With an inner urge to explore.
Skipping from limb to rock to land,
Handling moss and leaf and sand.
Catching frogs, lizards, fish and such,
Throwing stones – getting wet too much.

Brooks run shallow – brooks run deep.
Boyhood memories are bound to keep.

When a boy leaves this wonderland,
Another comes to take his stand.
Following the familiar ways,
By playing games and making waves.
So, fathers and sons both can share
Mysteries of these times so fair.

Brooks run shallow – brooks run deep.
Boyhood memories are bound to keep.

Spring Flowers

Lilacs on the hillside.
Pussy willows in the dell.
Tulips in the garden.
Crocuses by the well.

Blood Root in the forest.
Jack in the Pulpit by the pond.
Marsh Marigolds near the brook.
The ferns grow hither and yon.

Bluets edge the meadow.
White clover through the lawn.
Low phlox grace the stonewall.
Buttercups break at dawn.

Dogwood in the valley.
Blue Bells on the slope.
Blossoms in the orchard.
The Violets give us hope.
      BUT THE
Lily of the Valley is my favorite
With each bloom heaven made
Spreading joy and gladness
With all its scents of shade.

Shadows on the Garden Wall

The shadows on the garden wall
Happen just at the evenfall,
Marking twilight as I recall,
These shadows on the garden wall.

Coming together to make one,
Forming images on the run
As they move along with the sun.
These shadows on the garden wall.

Long ones – short ones – in between
Thin ones – stout ones – with image keen,
Such a tranquil romantic scene,
These shadows on the garden wall.

Silhouettes on stone of gray
At the passing of the day
But only for a moment stay
These shadows on the garden wall.

Catching these shadows with delight,
Your heart will be warmed with the sight,
Bringing your day to close just right.
These shadows on the garden wall.

The Old Stonewall

Built by farmers in the days of yore
From the plowed-up rocks and stones galore,
Lying there a hundred years or more,
The old stonewall.

Stacked just right one over two at first,
Then two over one – just in reverse,
Over and over as if rehearsed,
The old stone wall.

Dividing forest and pasture green,
Standing there staunch and strong in between,
Creating a most pictorial scene.
The old stonewall.

Home to chipmunk, rabbit, mouse, and snake,
A comfortable place it doth create.
From outside danger it gives a break.
The old stonewall.

A place where the local children play
Standing, or jumping with hearts so gay
As bonding friendships are cast in clay.
The old stonewall

It may seem a relic old and gray,
But it works its magic every day,
Not as silent as it might portray.
The old stonewall.

The Winds on Secore's Hill

The winds up on Secore's Hill,
Are almost never ever still.
They sweep up from down below,
Tossing objects to and fro.

The scene within Old Bill's farm,
Would give lesser men alarm,
But Bill takes it all in stride
Never one to go and hide.

As the trees are bent and bare,
From the currents in the air
The leaf and the blade ascend,
Seemingly to never end.

When the children play outside,
Securely, they must be tied.
To keep them down on the ground,
Instead of being upward bound.

The dogs, cats and smaller pets,
Float around and never set.
They will all tumble up and down,
And then over and around.

Depending upon their size,
Farm animals may arise.
The cows and sheep and the goat,
May just stay or go afloat.

The poor chickens have no chance,
To the sky they will advance.
Churning over and around
Until they all come back down.

As the farm pond rises high,
The fish and frogs get to fly,
When they finally descend,
They know not to where they end.

When the winds have had their blow
And decide it's time to go,
Everything falls out of space,
Dropping to its former place.

And as the winds do subside,
Gravity's laws will abide.
Then all is well as before
On the farm of Bill Secore

Fireflies

Daylight failing.
Darkness hailing.
Summer night prevailing.

First a flash,
Then a dash.
Just a few and then a rash.

Willful prancing.
Joyous dancing.
Night scenes unfold romancing.

Darts of light
Through the night,
Here and there and out of sight.

Fading night.
Dawning light,
Out of mind and out of sight.

The Old Swimming Hole

The old swimming hole is now gone,
A shallow bog stands in its place,
Still, some of us do remember
From the days of our youthful grace.

On those warm sunlit summer days,
We all centered around its charm.
Days full of fun and frolicking
That we spent out upon the farm.

Jumping in off the old oak plank
That protruded out from the shore,
Or swinging down from hanging vines
Then plunging to the muddy floor.

While falling in and out of love
With all the girls that lived nearby;
Running, chasing, jumping, swimming
As youthful summers flew on by.

Playing among wild flowers.
Chasing butterflies white and gold.
Catching tadpoles, fish and lizards
Never thinking we'd e'er grow old.

Though the old swimming hole is gone,
Deep in our minds it lingers still
Leaving pictures of bygone days,
Giving our hearts a lasting thrill.

The Cherry Thieves

The night is dark – the moon is low,
With bags in hand and hearts aglow,
They're walking down the orchard row.

Moving on toward the barn of white,
They're staying low and out of sight,
These robbers of the slumber night.

With cherry trees before them now,
They spot the fruit on bended bough,
Planning to get to them somehow.

Then up the tree they move with ease,
With breaking bark and rustling leaves,
These hearty youths – these cherry thieves.

Filling their bags with lush red fruit,
Quietly done with movements mute,
Excitedly they steal the loot.

All is well on this eve so dark,
Until a dog begins to bark,
Quickly ending their merry lark.

As howling sounds are everywhere,
Down from the tree they jump with care,
These bandits of the cool night air.

Through orchard grass they run their race,
With youthful speed and deer like grace.
Out of danger they slow their pace.

Safely away and out of sight,
With spoils in hand their hearts are light,
These robbers of the slumber night.

Lulabelle

When I first met Lulabelle,
She was walking home from town.
Dressed in clothes made from burlap,
And other scrapes she found.

She walked the old mountain road
To town at least twice a week
To buy necessities, whiskey,
And a few other things to eat.

The last mile of her journey
Was uphill all the way,
But it brought her to her mountain home,
Where she loved to stay.

I often wondered what made her live
In this difficult and daunting place,
Perhaps it was the call of the wind
As it blew through the open space.

When she grew older
And the town officials had their way,
They placed her in an old folks' home,
And there they made her stay.

But as you may well imagine,
She didn't stay there long.
She gathered up her belongings,
Opened the door, and she was gone.

A few days later I saw her
Walking the old road once more
On her way to town
To buy a few things at the store.

On that cold and snowy evening
As she climbed toward the home she left,
She decided to sit awhile
And there she froze to death.

I remember you, Lulabelle,
For the defiant spirit you had
I guess that's why
You had a smile on your face. NOT SAD!

Death of a Great Poet

He never wrote a sonnet,
Nor composed a poet's song,
And he never wrote in verse,
Nor recited to a throng.

And yet he was a poet,
As sure as autumn leaves fall.
His life was his poetry,
Touching all the hearts he saw.

He walked through lonesome valleys,
And he danced beneath the stars.
He followed the garden paths,
With the wind he had his spars.

He talked with little children,
He made music with the bees,
He found favor with the birds,
And he laughed among the trees.

At his funeral no one wept,
Although everyone was there.
His friends knew of his nature,
His life was beyond compare.

Yes, he was a great poet.
His actions sang through his song.
When he arrived in heaven,
They all knew that he belonged.

Can I Go Out Fishing in Heaven?

Can I go out fishing in heaven or only here on earth?
I hope there is fishing in heaven, for whatever it's worth.
Since most of my fishing pals have moved to the great beyond,
I hope they've found solace at the water's edge by river — by pond.
When I arrive with rod and reel in hand and a heart full of joy,
Will my pals be waiting or is fishing in heaven a ploy?
Will we all be equipped with canoes, paddles, nets and the like?
Ready for a day on the water catching perch, catfish and pike?

At the end of a day out fishing when the sun has gone down,
Will we be swapping old stories about the big ones we found?
And then in our sweet dreams as we lay our heads down to rest,
Will our minds be full of fishing tales of only the best?
Maybe there is fishing in heaven, the more that I speak.
Why wouldn't there be, for heaven is certainly not bleak.
For Jesus loved all the fishermen that he found by the shore:
Simon Peter, James, John, Andrew and probably more.

When we are out fishing by land or out in an old boat,
Along the Sea of Galilee or by lake or river afloat.
Our hearts are pure and free from strife and prejudice and sin,
Strengthened way down in our souls with a quiet calmness within.

Stray Cat

I know not what you were,
Or how you came to be.
I only know you now,
And what you mean to me.

Starting as an acquaintance,
You're now a friend indeed.
Lifting me up in spirit,
Sharing my time of need.

So I give thanks for you,
When ere I stop to pray.
Thanks that you're with me,
And with me you will stay.

Little Yellow Chapel in the Grove

The Grove Chapel yellow and white
Doth form the most pictorial sight
On sacred ground by day and night,
Blessing the Grove with pure delight.

A bell that rings on Sunday morn
Welcomes the faithful to its charm,
With natural wood – stained glass adorned,
Giving a glow that's rich and warm.

This chapel in the wildwood
so perfectly there, understood
And praised by all of those who would
Be inspired by grace and good.

Many saints have passed through its door.
Some were famous but most obscure,
Preachers, teachers, tradesmen and more
Nurses, bankers, housewives for sure.

Although times have changed all and all,
The believers still seek the call
Responding to the chapel's draw
In summer, winter, spring, and fall.

Saints are blessed as in days of old,
Listening to the word unfold
And singing hymns with joy untold
In this chapel of yellow gold.

Twilight on the Hudson

Reflections upon the River
Created by the moon above
Shared with the dancing city lights,
Releasing airs of joy and love.

Ripples catching the beams of light
Sending them to the distant shore
While watchers on the other side
View a scene they can't ignore.

A Place Called Childhood

When I was a child,
I knew a place – a special place –
Hidden from the world outside.
A place where I could be myself
And never have to hide.

In this special place,
I had a name – a special name –
That fit me to a tee.
It made me feel good inside,
That special name for me.

Also in this place,
I had a friend – a special friend –
Imaginary but real.
Together we explored the earth,
By sea – by air – by wheel.

As I grew older,
I left this place – this special place –
To roam the whole world wide.
I took my name and my friend,
They're always by my side.

This Old Barn

If this old barn could spin a yarn,
Oh, what untold stories it could tell
Out of the days of yesteryear
From its perch way down in the dell.

Its creaking doors open early
Each morning at the crack of dawn
As the old farmer works yawning
Until all the milk has been drawn

Tales of milking time every day
With cows in stanchions in a row
And milking machines all attached
Letting life-giving liquids flow.

Then with the milking all complete
And everything's back in its place,
The farmer has time to relax,
To slow down, and slacken his pace.

Hot summer days at haying time
As the old loft begins to fill
With a large crop of good fresh hay
To get though the long winter chill.

Then children running and jumping
As only they know how to play
Flopping, tossing, rolling, falling,
Over and over in the hay.

With the bull pacing back and forth
While having a mischievous thought
Waiting for the chance to escape
To wreak havoc before he's caught.

The old barn cat chasing the mice
To keep their population down
Or the dog that barks in the night
When it hears a threatening sound.

Cows calving from day into night
As the newborns wobble or fall.
Then they gather balance just right
And begin to stand straight and tall.

As the old farmer cleans each stall
With a pitch fork, shovel, and rake,
He gently lays down some fresh straw
Improving the scent in its wake.

During the short days of winter
After dark with snow on the ground,
There's a warm glow through the windows
That's seen from outside all around.

As all of these stories unfold
Along with so-so many more,
This old barn with all of its charm
Is full of memories galore

The Ghost Herd

Thundering through the light at dawn
To the horizon they are drawn.
Blacks, Whites, and Buckskins tawn,
These phantoms ever charging on.

Over the plains and prairie grass
At a gallop that's quick and fast
Blue Roans, Strawberries, Chestnuts alas,
These sacred wild shadows pass.

Onward they advance the chase
At a blazingly rapid pace.
Pintos, bays, dapple grays bald face,
They carry on with mystic grace.

As twilight fades into the west,
They move on toward the skyline crest.
Sorrels, paints, grays, and all the rest,
These wild ghosts so heaven blessed.

The Temple Green

When I am sad and lonely,
And my heart is full of pain,
I seek the green wood only,
Strolling down the Lord's own lane.

The path is not straight at all,
It winds through the green and brown.
As I stumble – as I fall,
There I lay my burdens down.

The birds sing songs of gladness.
Wildflowers grow at my feet.
They take away my sadness,
Putting sorrows in retreat.

Spring waters splash around me,
Weaving through moss-laden rock.
Gentle cleansing abounds me,
Shattering misfortune's lock.

Through the temple he walks with me,
And shares my load awhile.
Comforted by the green I see,
I am brightened by his smile.

www.ingramcontent.com/pod-product-compliance
Lightning Source LLC
Chambersburg PA
CBHW061146010526
44118CB00026B/2885